Languages of the World

Japanese

Harriet Milles

Heinemann
LIBRARY

Chicago, Illinois

www.capstonepub.com
Visit our website to find out more information about Heinemann-Raintree books.

To order:
☎ Phone 888-454-2279
▣ Visit www.capstonepub.com to browse our catalog and order online.

© 2012 Heinemann Library
an imprint of Capstone Global Library, LLC
Chicago, Illinois

Edited by Dan Nunn and Diyan Leake
Designed by Marcus Bell
Original illustrations © Capstone Global Library Ltd 2012
Picture research by Elizabeth Alexander

Originated by Capstone Global Library Ltd
Printed and bound in China by South China Printing
 Company Ltd

15 14 13 12 11
10 9 8 7 6 5 4 3 2 1

Library of Congress Cataloging-in-Publication Data

Milles, Harriet.
  Japanese / Harriet Milles.—1st ed.
     p. cm.—(Languages of the world)
  Text in English and Japanese.
  Includes bibliographical references and index.
  ISBN 978-1-4329-5836-7—ISBN 978-1-4329-5844-2 (pbk.)
  1. Japanese language—Textbooks for foreign speakers—
English. 2. Japanese language—Grammar. 3. Japanese
language—Spoken Japanese. I. Title.
  PL539.5.E5M55 2012
  495.6'82421—dc23   2011017916

Acknowledgments
The author and publisher are grateful to the following for permission to reproduce copyright material: Alamy pp. 5 (© Alex Segre), 6 (© Photo Resource Hawaii), 13 (© amana images inc.), 22 (© John Cole), 23 (© amana images inc.); Getty Images pp. 8 (MIXA), 21 (MIXA); iStockphoto pp. 7 (© Stephan Hoerold), 16 (© Christine Glade); Photolibrary pp. 18 (Klaus-Werner Friedrich), 24 (JTB Photo); Shutterstock pp. 9 (© discpicture), 11 (© Mandy Godbehear), 12 (© grafica), 14 (© mamahoohooba), 15 (© AVAVA), 17 (© paulaphoto), 19 (© Steve Yager), 20 (© Monkey Business Images), 25 (© J. Henning Buchholz), 26 (© bonchan), 27 (© svry), 28 (© Jose AS Reyes), 29 (© takayuki).

Cover photograph reproduced with permission of Alamy (© MIXA).

Every effort has been made to contact copyright holders of material reproduced in this book. Any omissions will be rectified in subsequent printings if notice is given to the publisher.

Contents

Japanese words in this book are in italics, *like this*. You can find out how to say them by looking in the pronunciation guide.

What Do You Know About Japanese?

Japanese is the language of the country of Japan, in Asia. Japanese people call their country *Nippon*, which means "Land of the Rising Sun." They call their language *Nihongo*.

Japan is a country of four main islands and many smaller islands.

Japan

This is a busy street in Tokyo. Tokyo is the capital city of Japan.

Politeness is very important in Japan. Children speak differently to adults than to their friends. People speak differently at work than at home.

Who Speaks Japanese?

Japan is the only country in the world where Japanese is the main language. Many Japanese-speaking people also live in Hawaii, which is part of the United States.

Some people born in Hawaii have Japanese parents or grandparents.

About 127 million people live in Japan.

There are Japanese-speaking people in Brazil and Peru in South America, too. Japanese is fun to learn! Are you ready to speak some Japanese?

Reading and Writing in Japanese

Japanese people write in "characters," or scripts. They use three different reading and writing systems. *Kanji* and *hiragana* are the most commonly used systems.

Japanese children must learn to read and write 1,006 characters before they leave elementary school!

私　*kanji*

わたし　*hiragana*

ワタシ　*katakana*

> Here is the Japanese word for "I" (*watashi*) written in the different scripts.

Katakana is mostly used for names and non-Japanese words. Japanese characters can seem difficult to English-speaking people. Don't worry! Turn the page to find an easy way to learn Japanese.

Learning Japanese

People who are learning Japanese for the first time will usually be taught in *romaji*. In *romaji*, Japanese words are written in the same alphabet that is used to write English.

Japanese character	Romaji	How to say it	English
山	yama	ya-ma	mountain
おいしい	oishii	oy-shee	nice, tasty
テレビ	terebi	te-re-bi	television

These are Japanese words that are written in letters of the English alphabet.

How to say it
English = *Eigo*
What does that mean? = *Kore wan an to yuu imi desu ka?*
please = *onegai shimasu*
thank you = *arigato gozaimasu*

Romaji helps you to know how Japanese characters should sound. You may already know some *romaji*! If you or your friends go to *judo* or *karate* classes, you use Japanese words.

11

Saying Hello and Goodbye

Japanese people usually greet each other by bowing. They may say, "*Konnichiwa!*" to greet a friend, or "*Hajimemashite*" ("It's nice to meet you") if they are meeting someone for the first time.

How to say it
hello = *konnichiwa*
It's nice to
meet you =
Hajimemashite

How to say it
goodbye (leaving for a long time) = *sayonara*
good morning = *ohayougozaimasu*
good evening = *konbanwa*
good night = *oyasuminasai*

The Japanese say, "*Moshi, moshi!*" ("Speak, speak!") when they answer the telephone. There are different ways to say goodbye. *Itte kimasu* means "Goodbye, see you later."

Talking About Yourself

When you meet people for the first time, they will usually ask what your name is. Then you may say, "*Watashi no namae wa ... desu*" ("My name is ...").

How to say it
My name is Yuko = *Watashi no namae wa Yuko desu*

They may ask you where you live. You can say, "*Watashi wa … ni sunde imasu*" ("I live in …"), or "*Watashi wa … kara kimashita*" ("I come from …").

Asking About Others

If you want to ask someone's name, you can say, "*Anata no namae wa nan desu ka?*" ("What is your name?").

How to say it
What is your name = *Anata no namae wa nan desu ka?*

To find out where someone comes from, you may say, "*Doko kara kimashita ka?*" ("Where are you from?"), or "*Doko ni sunde imasu ka?*" ("Where do you live?")

At Home

Japanese homes usually have a kitchen, a bathroom, a separate area for a toilet, and one or two rooms for living. People never wear shoes indoors. They take them off at the door.

How to say it
home = *uchi*
kitchen = *kitchin*
bathroom = *ofuro*
toilet = *toire*

How to say it
living room = *ima*
bed = *beddo* or *futon*

Traditional Japanese homes have mats called *tatami* on the floor. The family members sit on cushions, not chairs. At night they sleep on the floor on special mattresses called *futon*.

Family

Japanese families are generally small, with just one or two children. Sometimes grandparents live with the family, too. In springtime, families go on picnics to enjoy the cherry blossoms.

How to say it

family = *kazoku*   father = *chichi*

mother = *haha*   grandparents = *sofubo*

Families do things together on special festival days and holidays. On Children's Day (*Kodomo no hi*), boys fly kites shaped like fish. On Girls' Day (*Hina matsuri*), families display dolls.

At School

Japanese schools start at 8:30 a.m. and finish at around 4:00 p.m. Children learn how to read and write in the different types of Japanese characters. They also learn math, history, and science.

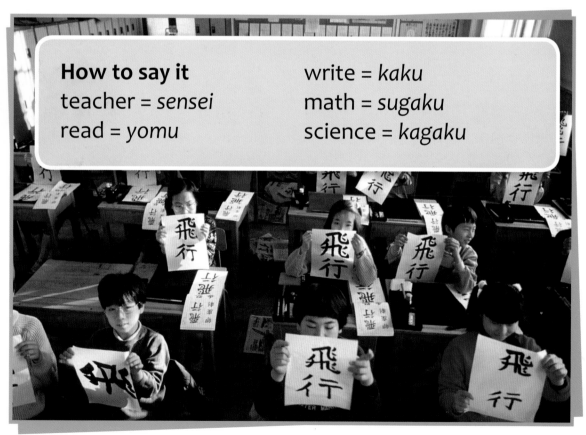

How to say it
teacher = *sensei*
read = *yomu*
write = *kaku*
math = *sugaku*
science = *kagaku*

How to say it
class = *kurasu*
school = *gakko*
student = *seito*
learn = *manabu*
clean = *soujisuru*

After lunch, all the children clean the school. Then they may play sports or do other activities, such as music or dancing. They may have more classes or a study period.

Sports and Leisure

Japan is famous for martial arts. These are fighting sports, such as *judo*, *karate*, and *kendo*. Children in Japan start to learn one of these arts at a young age.

How to say it
sports = *supotsu*

How to say it
soccer = *sakka*
team = *chimu*
ball = *boru*

The national sport of Japan is sumo wrestling. Soccer, baseball, surfing, and skiing are also popular sports. In their free time, Japanese children love to read *manga* (comic books).

Food

Rice, noodles, and fish are popular foods in Japan. Breakfast may be a bowl of rice with soup and an egg, or some fish. All meals are eaten with chopsticks.

How to say it
rice = *gohan*
noodles = *men*
chopsticks = *o-hashi*

A popular lunchtime meal is noodles with vegetables, seaweed, and fish. A Japanese lunchbox is called a *bento*. Some stores sell pre-packaged *bento* for people to take with them.

Clothes

Most Japanese people relax in T-shirts and jeans. They wear more formal clothes for work. People love color in Japan! Some teenagers wear a brightly colored style of clothes called *decora*.

How to say it
T-shirt = *T-shatsu*
jeans = *jinzu*
shoes = *kutsu*
socks = *kutsushita*
skirt = *sukato*

People wear *kimono* with a wide sash called an *obi*.

For special occasions, people may dress in a traditional Japanese robe called a *kimono*. They will wear special sandals called *zori* on their feet.

Pronunciation Guide

English	Romaji	Pronunciation
bathroom	*ofuro*	*o-**fu**-ro*
bed	*beddo or futon*	***bed**-do/fu-**ton***
breakfast	*asa-gohan*	*a-**sa**-**go**-han*
brother	*ototo (younger)/ani (older)*	*o-**toh**-to/**a**-ni*
chopsticks	*o-hashi*	*o-**ha**-shi*
class	*kurasu*	***ku**-ra-s*
clean	*souji-suru*	***saw**-ji-su-ru*
dinner	*ban-gohan*	*ban-**go**-han*
English	*Eigo*	***ay**-go*
family	*kazoku*	***ka**-zo-ku*
father	*chichi*	*chi-**chi***
fish	*sakana*	*sa-**ka**-na*
good evening	*konbanwa*	*kon-**ban**-wa*
good morning	*ohayougozaimasu*	*o-**ha**-**yoh**-go-zai-mas*
good night	*oyasuminasai*	*o-**ya**-su-**mi**-na-sai*
goodbye	*sayonara (for a long time)/ itte kimasu (leaving the house)*	*sa-**yoh**-**na**-ra/ it-**te** **ki**-ma-s*
grandparents	*sofubo*	*so-**fu**-bo*
hello	*konnichiwa*	*kon-**ni**-**chi**-**wa***
holiday	*yasumi*	*ya-**su**-**mi***
home	*uchi*	*ooh-**chi***
I come from …	*Watashi wa … kara kimashita*	*wa-**ta**-**shi** wa … **ka**-ra ki-**ma**-**shi**-**ta***
I live in …	*Watashi wa … ni sunde imasu*	*wa-**ta**-**shi** wa … ni **su**-n-de i-ma-s*
It's nice to meet you	*Hajimemashite*	*ha-**ji**-**me**-**ma**-**shi**-tih*
Japanese	*Nihongo*	*ni-**hon**-go*
jeans	*jinzu*	***jee**-n-zu*
kitchen	*kitchin*	***kit**-chin*
learn	*manabu*	*ma-**na**-bu*

living room	*ima*	i-**ma**
lunch	*hiru-gohan*	hi-**ru-go**-han
math	*sugaku*	su-**ga-ku**
mother	*haha*	**ha**-ha
My name is ...	*Watashi no namae wa ... desu*	wa-**ta-shi** no na-**ma-e** wa ... des
noodles	*men*	**men**
please	*onegai shimasu*	o-**ne-gai shi**-mas
read	*yomu*	**yo**-mu
rice	*gohan*	**go**-han
school	*gakko*	gak-**koh**
science	*kagaku*	**ka**-ga-ku
shoes	*kutsu*	ku-**tsu**
sister	*imoto* (younger)/*ane* (older)	ih-**moh-to**/**a**-nih
skirt	*sukato*	su-**kah-to**
soccer	*sakka*	**sak**-kah
socks	*kutsushita*	ku-**tsu-shi-ta**
sports	*supotsu*	su-**poh**-ts
student	*seito*	**say**-to
T-shirt	*T-shatsu*	T-**sha**-ts
teacher	*sensei*	sen-**say**
team	*chimu*	**chee**-mu
thank you	*arigato gozaimasu*	a-**ri**-ga-toh go-**zai**-mas
toilet	*toire*	**toy**-re
What does that mean?	*Kore wa nan to yuu imi desu ka?*	ko-**re wa nan** to yuu i-mi des **ka**
What is your name?	*Anata no namae wa nan desu ka?*	a-**na-ta** no na-**ma-e** wa **nan** des **ka**
Where are you from?	*Doko kara kimashita ka?*	**do**-ko ka-ra ki-**ma-shi-ta ka**
Where do you live?	*Doko ni sunde imasu ka?*	**do**-ko ni **su**-n-de i--mas **ka**
write	*kaku*	**ka**-ku

1 = chi, 2 = ni, 3 = san, 4 = shi, 5 = go, 6 = roku, 7 = shichi, 8 = hachi, 9 = kyu, 10 = ju

Find Out More

Books

Galan, Christian, and Florence Lerot-Calvo. *I'm Learning Japanese!: A Language Adventure for Young People*. North Clarendon, Vt.: Tuttle, 2010.

Phillips, Charles. *Japan* (Countries of the World). Washington, D.C.: National Geographic, 2009.

Sato, Eriko, and Anna Sato. *My First Japanese Kanji Book: Learning Kanji the Fun and Easy Way!* North Clarendon, Vt.: Tuttle, 2009.

Websites

http://library.thinkquest.org/CR0212302/japan.html

http://web-jpn.org/kidsweb/language

http://kids.asiasociety.org/explore/childrens-day-japan-kodomo-no-hi

Index